What Do Kids Need to Know About Finance?

Leslie Anne Perry, Ph.D.

Timothy T. (Ty) Perry, Ph.D.

Illustrated by
Nathan Dunnavant

Long, long ago kids did not need to know anything about what we now call finance. And neither did grown-ups. In fact, if you had lived then, you would not even have had money. Because long, long ago people gathered, or hunted, or grew, or made just about everything they needed. In other words, they were self-sufficient.

Sometimes, though, people found they needed things they could not make or find. In order to get things they needed, they traded something they had for something another person had. Trading to get items they needed or wanted was called bartering.

Have you ever traded something you had with a friend who gave you something he or she had? When people trade goods or services but are not paid any money, they are bartering. Even today people barter.

Long ago bartering worked well for many people. But it was also a lot of trouble. Maybe a man raised pigs and wanted to trade a pig for some grain. He would have to find someone with extra grain who would trade it for a pig. Trying to find someone who had what you needed, and was willing to trade it for something you had, could take a long time. And deciding how much an item was worth was often hard.

Even in ancient times, people began using various items as money. Smaller items that were durable and easy to carry worked best. These were often small items made of gold, copper, or bronze. Shells, beads, feathers, and even salt were sometimes used as money long ago.

In order for people to use an item for money, other people needed to agree what that item was worth. A piece of metal might have a different value to different people. To make things easier, around 2700 years ago, people in Turkey began making coins out of metal. Each coin had the amount it was worth stamped on it. Metal coins made buying things much easier.

Since the United States first started making coins, the coins have changed many times. Today our coins have pictures of former presidents on them. They also have other pictures and information. It is interesting to look at U.S. coins to see what information they contain.

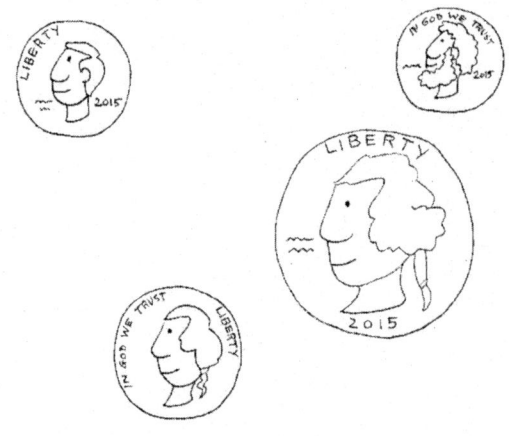

Paper money is less durable than coins, but it is lighter weight and much easier to carry. In the 13 original states, paper money was different in each of the states. During the Revolutionary War, the Continental Congress issued paper money.

During the Civil War, both the northern states and the southern states had their own money. In order to finance the Civil War, the United States issued what could be called the first national currency.

Today in the United States we have paper money in these amounts: $1, $5, $10, $20, $50, $100. The paper money used in each of the 50 states is the same. This means the dollar bills people spend in one state look just like the dollar bills people spend in the other 49 states.

Most kids have no trouble spending money. There are so many things to spend money on. And there are so many places to spend it.

Spending money is much easier than saving money. And most kids would probably agree it is a whole lot more fun.

To keep track of where you are spending your money, you could use a small notebook. In the notebook, you could write down each thing you buy and how much it cost. If you do this for three months or more, you will get a good idea of where your money is being spent.

When thinking about what people spend money on, it is helpful to separate things into wants and needs. You may have heard there are only three things people really need: food, clothing, and shelter. Actually, water should be added to the food category. Your body must have both food and water in order for you to stay alive.

As for clothing, it depends on where you live when thinking about the type of clothing you need. Most people would agree that walking around naked in public is probably not a good idea. But, beyond covering your body, clothing needs vary from place to place. They also vary with the time of year if you live in a place with four seasons.

Needs related to shelter vary also. Sleeping outside under the stars might work for people who live in very warm climates. It might also work for a warm summer night in a place that is not warm all year long. But, if it starts to rain, you probably would not be too comfortable outside. Some type of shelter, a home of some kind, would be good to have.

A need is something you must have, like food, clothing, and shelter. And most people like their shelter to have electricity, water, and a source of heat when it is cold. But other things people spend money on are really things they want, not things they need. You could still go on living if you did not buy something you wanted but did not actually need.

Do you really, really need a new video game that is way cooler than the ones you already have? Actually you don't. You want it. And it may provide many hours of fun. But a video game is a want, not a need.

No one would say, however, that you should never, ever buy items you simply want. It is alright to want to buy things you do not really need. Everybody buys things they can do without, but that they would like to have.

In managing your spending, it is a good idea to think about what you want the most. Then you can make that particular purchase a goal you are working toward. Sometimes an item costs more money than you have. This may mean you will have to save your money until you have enough to buy that item.

Do you have a piggy bank or other special place to save money? A lot of kids do. Even grown-ups often have special places they put money when they want to save it. Some people even hide it under their mattress!

Sometimes you want to save larger amounts of money than you want to keep in your house. You may choose to put it in a bank. This may be safer than keeping money in your house. Also, money you save in a bank can earn interest. Money in your piggy bank cannot.

Have you heard the saying "saving for a rainy day?" You can also save for a windy day, a snowy day, and a hot, sunny day! "Saving for a rainy day" does not have anything to do with the weather. It just means saving for unexpected things.

Kids also save money so they can buy items they want or need. Grown-ups do this too. And grown-ups save money so they will have enough to live on after they retire and are no longer working.

As we said, you can earn interest when you put your money in a bank. The amount of interest you earn is based on the interest rate the bank offers. The amount of interest a bank pays will be less than the amount of interest a bank charges people when it lends them money. That is because a bank is in the business of making money.

Maybe you have saved $50 and you have opened a savings account at a bank. If your bank pays 1% interest, that would be 50¢. That does not sound like much. But, each time the interest is added, you will have more money in your account. Over time, the amount of money in your account will keep increasing.

If a family lives in a house or apartment that is owned by someone else, they usually pay rent. Many people would rather buy a house than pay rent for a long period of time. But, for most grown-ups, a house costs more money than they would earn in several years. Saving money to pay cash for a house could take a very long time.

In order to go ahead and buy a house, many grown-ups borrow money from a bank. A house loan is called a mortgage.

When someone borrows money to buy a house, they sign a contract. The contract includes information about the amount of the loan and how it must be paid back. The person who borrows the money usually has to pay a down payment. Then they pay a certain amount each month until the money is paid back.

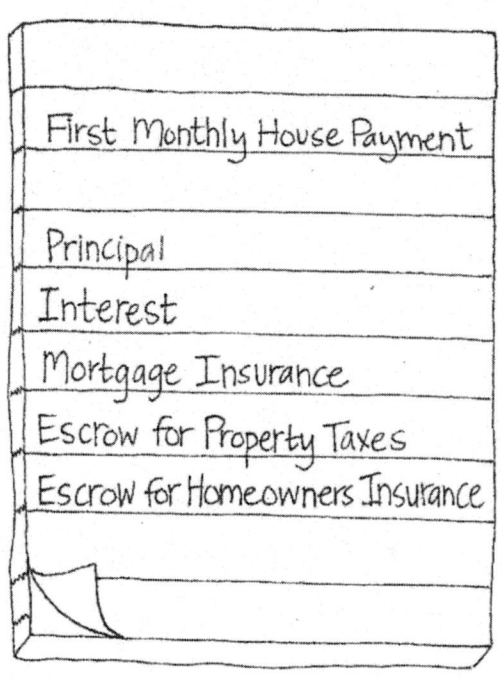

Banks do not lend money to people just to help them out. They lend money because that is one of the ways they make money. Banks charge people interest on the money that is borrowed.

When someone makes a monthly mortgage payment to a bank, the payment will include an amount for both the principal and the interest. The principal part of the payment is the part that goes toward paying off the loan. The interest part of the payment goes to the bank for the use of their money. Part of a mortgage payment may also be for insurance and property taxes.

Most people put their money in a bank rather than hide it somewhere. Their money is safer in a bank. And it can earn interest there. But banks do more than offer a place for people to save money and earn interest. And they do more than lend money to people and charge them interest.

One of the services banks offer is checking accounts. The way a checking account works is that a person deposits money into an account. Then, when they need to use some of that money, they write a check. Writing a check is sort of like writing a letter to the bank to tell them to take a certain amount of money out of your account. Money can also be transferred from one account to another without a check being written. Online banking allows people to send money to pay bills, etc., and eliminates the need to write paper checks.

Many people use debit cards in addition to, or instead of, writing checks. You may have been shopping with a grown-up who used a small, plastic card to pay for something. The person at the cash register may have asked "debit or credit?" They were asking if the card being used was a debit card or a credit card. If the card is a debit card, after the card is slid through a card reader, the amount owed will be deducted from the person's checking account.

Using a debit card is sort of like writing a check. You are telling the bank to take a certain amount of money out of your account. But the transfer of money is made possible immediately when you slide the card through a card reader and key in a PIN (Personal Identification Number).

Credit cards are another service offered by banks. When people use credit cards, they are not telling the bank to use money from their account. Instead, they are actually borrowing money from the bank. And, since one of the ways banks make money is by charging interest, the bank charges for this service.

You may have been shopping with a grown-up who used a credit card to pay for something. After the card was slid through the card reader, the amount of the purchase was added to the amount owed on the credit card.

Paying the bank back for credit card purchases can be done over a period of time by making monthly payments. Or it can be paid back all at once. The longer the money is owed to the bank, the greater the amount of interest that will have to be paid.

If everyone wanted to take their money out of a bank at the same time, there would not be enough money for everyone. This is because a lot of the money a bank takes in is loaned out to people to buy houses, cars, or other things. And it is loaned out to people when they make purchases using a credit card issued by that bank.

A credit union is like a bank in that it offers savings accounts, checking accounts, and loans. However, a credit union is a not-for-profit financial institution. Any profits it makes are given back to its members as dividends.

A credit union is actually owned by its members, and it is governed by a board of directors elected by the members. Also, members of a credit union have some type of connection to each other. For example, they may all be teachers in a particular region. Or they may all be employees of the same large company.

A savings bank offers savings accounts, checking accounts, and loan services like a bank or a credit union. A savings bank may also be called a savings and loan.

Savings banks specialize in real estate financing. This means that they are heavily involved in lending money to people who want to buy houses or other properties.

When people invest their money, they put it somewhere that it can make money, or grow in value over time. In other words, the idea behind investing is to make money with your money.

Pretend you and a friend have decided to start a dog walking business. You have figured out you can each walk three dogs at once. To start your business, you take money out of your savings and buy six sturdy dog leashes. The new leashes will make it easier for you to each manage three dogs at once.

For your dog walking business, you may be walking dogs in very cold weather. So you take more money from your savings to buy warm hats and warm gloves. These items, along with the new dog leashes, are your investment in your dog walking business.

Soon your neighbors realize you are dependable and will do a good job walking their dogs each day. So they agree to pay you for doing this. But, before you can know how much you are earning in your business, you will need to subtract the amount of your investment. Once you have earned enough to cover your investment, you will begin making a profit.

When grown-ups invest money, they also want to make money with their money. They might ask themselves these questions: (1) Is this a safe place to put my money? (2) Am I going to make money on this investment? The goal of investing is to use your money to make money. So an investment that is worth less when you take your money out is not a very good investment.

Some grown-ups invest money in stock. They may do this through a company that invests money for people. Sometimes grown-ups invest in stock through a retirement account. The purpose of a retirement account is to earn money in order to have more money in the future.

When people invest money in stock it means they own a portion of the company that issued the stock. Someone who owns a large number of shares of stock in a company has more ownership in that company than a person who owns a small number of shares. In the past, when people bought stock, they were issued a stock certificate. The certificate showed how many shares they owned. Today, this information is recorded electronically.

Stock is usually bought and sold through a stock exchange. Most people agree that the first stock exchange was the one that opened in 1602 in Amsterdam, Holland. Today, there are stock exchanges all over the world. One of the largest is the New York Stock Exchange (NYSE).

In the past, stock was bought or sold by brokers on the trading floor of the exchange itself. Today, a large number of transactions take place over the Internet or by telephone.

If a company who issued the stock makes a lot of money, the stockholders may receive dividends. And the value of their stock may increase. But, if a company loses a lot of money, the stockholders are not likely to earn money on their investment.

Money problems can occur when the money a person has coming in (income) is less than what they need. This can happen to just about anybody, at any time. But sometimes not having enough money coming in can be much more serious. For example, when people lose their jobs, they often do not have enough money for the things they must have.

Sometimes when grown-ups have serious money problems, they can no longer make payments to the bank that loaned them money to buy their house. If they will not be able to make payments for quite a while, the bank may foreclose on the house. This means the bank then owns the house. It no longer belongs to the people who bought it.

People who lose their homes because they can no longer make payments may have to rely on family members or others to help them out. Even in very difficult times, there are often people who are willing to help people who are in need.

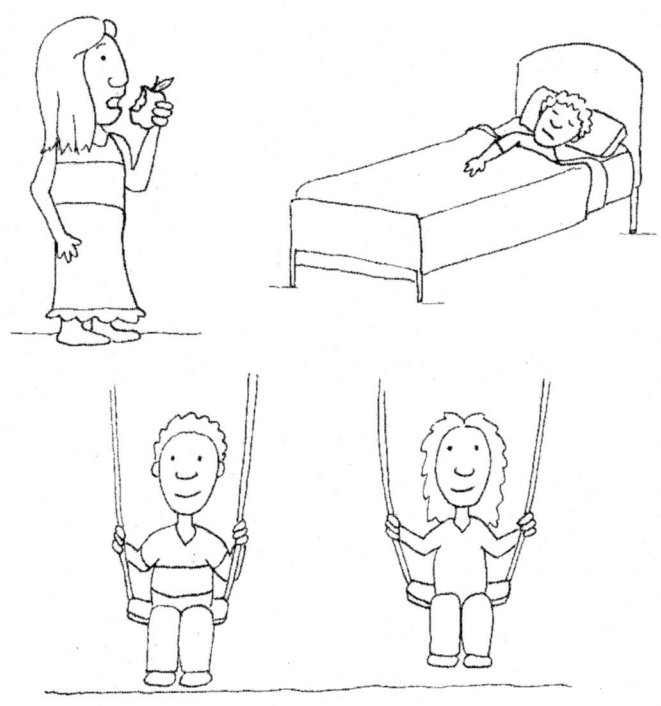

So, what do kids need to know about finance? They need to know that money is a part of all our lives. And they need to know that even kids can work toward managing money wisely.

Financial health is sort of like physical health. You can work toward being physically healthy by eating healthy foods, getting exercise, and getting enough sleep. You can also work toward good health by avoiding unhealthy habits and activities.

To be financially healthy, you need to work toward developing good habits and attitudes relating to money. You may have heard the saying "money can't buy happiness." Some of the happiest people are happy not because they have bunches and bunches of money. They are happy because they have been successful at living within their means. In other words, they manage their money rather than let their money manage them.

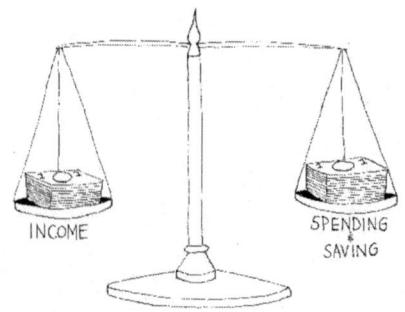

By starting early, and making wise decisions about spending and saving money, you can develop the habit of managing your money wisely.

Everyone, including kids, needs to balance the money they have coming in with the money they have going out. If you get an allowance, you can decide how much of that money you are going to spend. And you can decide how much you are going to save. You can even open a savings account at a bank.

By saving some of your money you can see your savings grow over time. Then, when you want something really special, you may just have enough money to buy it all by yourself. And that, too, is pretty special.

Glossary

ATM: Automated Teller Machine or Automatic Teller Machine, machine where people can make deposits and withdraw money from their bank accounts

bank: a for-profit business corporation that offers a range of financial services, including opportunities for saving and borrowing money

barter: trading of goods or services between people when no money is exchanged

borrowing money: usually means getting money from a bank or other financial institution that will be paid back over a period of time through regular payments

checking account: account at a bank, or other financial institution, that allows a person to access his/her money by writing checks or using a debit card

closing costs: extra money paid at the time a house or other property is purchased

compound interest: when interest is added to the money a person has in an account, thus increasing the amount on which interest will be computed in the future

credit card: plastic card with a strip on the back which can be read if the card is slid through a card reader; when the card's user buys something with the card, the amount of the purchase is added to the amount owed from previous purchases

credit union: financial institution that is actually owned by its members who have access to a variety of services including savings accounts, checking accounts, and loans

debit card: a 3 3/8 inch by 2 1/8 inch plastic card with rounded corners that looks a lot like a credit card; debit cards differ from credit cards in that, when people use debit cards, they are accessing money they have in an account

down payment: amount of money people pay up front toward the purchase price when they are borrowing money to buy a house or other property

escrow: usually refers to money that is held in an account until it is needed for a specific purpose, such as to pay property taxes or to pay for homeowners insurance

equity: the portion of the value of a house or other property that the owner actually owns; the remaining portion is owned by whoever made the loan

financial institution: a bank, credit union, savings bank, or savings and loan that provides a variety of financial services such as savings accounts, checking accounts, and loans

foreclosure: when the ownership of a house or other property is taken back by the lender; usually occurs when payments are no longer being made

loan: money borrowed from another person or from a bank or other financial institution

income: money that a person has coming in; for many grown-ups under retirement age, the majority of their income is from the wages or salary they are paid for the work they do

interest: amount paid for the use of money borrowed from a bank or other financial institution, or the amount paid by a bank for the use of money people have in savings accounts

investment: usually means money paid for something with the expectation that it will increase in value and a profit will be made

mortgage: the loan on a house or other property

needs: things people absolutely cannot do without such as food (and water), clothing, and shelter

online banking: a service provided by banks, credit unions, and savings banks which enables most transactions to be completed online

principal: amount still owed on a loan; a portion of loan payments usually goes toward the principal, and some of the remaining portion is interest that goes to the lender for the use of the money

rent: money paid for using something that belongs to someone else; usually refers to money paid to live in a house or apartment owned by someone else

savings account: account with a bank or other financial institution where people can save money and earn interest on their money

savings bank: financial institution that offers a variety of services and specializes in lending money for the purchase of houses and other property

savings and loan: alternate name for a savings bank

stock: a share or shares of a corporation

stock exchange: a place where stocks and other securities are bought and sold

stock market: general term that refers to the buying and selling of stocks and other securities

About the Authors

Dr. Leslie Anne Perry, a former elementary teacher, is a professor emerita in the Clemmer College of Education at East Tennessee State University, where she taught children's literature and language arts classes for twenty years. She is the author or co-author of four traditionally published print books, nine self-published e-books, two tests, and sixty-eight articles in fifty-eight different journals and magazines.

Dr. Timothy T. (Ty) Perry has worked in the field of finance—first as a student, then as a faculty member—at universities in North Carolina, Tennessee, Texas, Mississippi, and Minnesota. Currently, he is an assistant professor of finance in the College of Business and Global Affairs at the University of Tennessee Martin. He has had articles published in the *Journal of Trading*, the *Review of Futures Markets*, the *Journal of International Finance Studies*, the *Global Business and Finance Review*, and the *Journal of Alternative Investments*.

About the Illustrator

Nathan Dunnavant is a native of Pulaski, Tennessee. Interested in art since childhood, he is a 2015 honors graduate of the University of Tennessee Martin where he took art classes and also prepared for a career as a teacher of special needs children. *What Do Kids Need to Know About Finance?* is his first children's book.

Copyright © 2015 by Perry Productions

All Rights Reserved

Cover Design by Dr. Tim Perry

ISBN-13: 978-1515181675
ISBN-10: 1515181677

Made in United States
North Haven, CT
01 May 2024

51977499R00022